discover countries

Discover
Brazil

Ed Parker

PowerKiDS press™

New York

Published in 2010 by The Rosen Publishing Group Inc.
29 East 21st Street, New York, NY 10010

Copyright © 2010 Wayland/The Rosen
Publishing Group, Inc.

First Edition

Concept design: Jason Billin
Editor: Susan Crean
Designer: Paul Manning
Consultant: Rob Bowden

Library of Congress Cataloging-in-Publication Data

Parker, Ed.
  Discover Brazil / Ed Parker.
      p. cm. -- (Discover countries)
  Includes index.
  ISBN 978-1-61532-286-2 (library binding)
  ISBN 978-1-61532-290-9 (paperback)
  ISBN 978-1-61532-291-6 (6-pack)
  1. Brazil--Juvenile literature. I. Title.
  F2508.5.P375 2010
  981--dc22

                    2009023731

Photographs:
t=top b=bottom 1, EASI-Images/Neal Cavalier-Smith; 3t, Shutterstock/Zina Seletskaya; 3b, Shutterstock/Maria Weidner;
4 (map), Stefan Chabluk; 5, Shutterstock/Celso Pupo; 6, EASI-Images/Ed Parker; 7, Shutterstock/Rafael Martin-Gaitero;
8, EASI-Images/Ed Parker; 9, EASI-Images/Ed Parker; 10, Shutterstock/Celso Pupo; 11, EASI-Images/Ed Parker;
12, EASI-Images/Ed Parker; 13, Shutterstock/Laurence Gough; 14, Ed Parker; 15, Mariordo; 16, EASI-Images/Ed Parker; 17,
Corbis/Jon Spaull; 18, Paulo Fridman/Bloomberg News/Landov/Photoshot; 19, Corbis/Pierre Merimée; 20,
EASI-Images/Ed Parker; 21, EASI-Images/Ed Parker; 22, EASI-Images/Ed Parker; 23, EASI-Images/Ed Parker;
24, EASI-Images/Ed Parker; 25, Shutterstock/Ricardo Manuel Silva de Sousa; 26, EASI-Images/Neal Cavalier-Smith;
-27t, Shutterstock/Rafael Martin-Gaitero; 27b, Shutterstock/Zina Seletskaya; 28, EASI-Images/Ed Parker;
29t, EASI-Images/Ed Parker; 29b, EASI-Images/Ed Parker.
Cover images: Mariordo, EASI-Images/Ed Parker

Manufactured in China
CPSIA Compliance Information: Batch #WAW0102PK: For Further Information
contact Rosen Publishing, New York, New York at 1-800-237-9932

Contents

Discovering Brazil 4

Landscape and climate 6

Population and health 8

Settlements and living 10

Family life 12

Religion and beliefs 14

Education and learning 16

Employment and economy 18

Industry and trade 20

Farming and food 22

Transportation and communications 24

Leisure and tourism 26

Environment and wildlife 28

Glossary 30

Topic web 31

Further Information, Web Sites,
    and Index 32

Discovering Brazil

Brazil is the fifth-largest country in the world, taking up nearly half the continent of South America. It is a land of extremes: big skyscrapers, plush American-style shopping malls—but also sprawling slums, rural poverty, and crime.

A country of regions

Brazil is made up of 26 states and an area called Brasilia where all the main government offices are based. It has five main geographical regions: the Amazon and Paraguay Basins, the Coastal Strip, and the Guianan and Brazilian Highlands. But the country is so large and the regions are so different that they are almost like separate countries.

Natural riches

Ever since Brazil became a Portuguese colony in 1500, its gold, precious stones, and natural resources have been a source of great wealth. Brazil's climate and soils are also good for growing cash crops. Portugal became rich on these exports until Brazil gained independence in 1890.

Brazil Statistics

Total area: 3,286,488 sq. miles (8,511,965 sq. km)
Capital city: Brasilia
Government type: Federal republic
Bordering countries: Argentina, Bolivia, Colombia, French Guiana, Guyana, Paraguay, Peru, Surinam, Uruguay, Venezuela
Currency: Real (R$)
Language: Portuguese

Modern Brazil

After World War II, the Brazilian government built a new capital city called Brasilia in the center of the country. The aim was to help unify Brazil by making it work like one big country rather than many independent states. During the same period, roads, railroads, ports, and airports were built to support business and industry. Today, Brazil is South America's most powerful country and one of the most dynamic developing economies in the world.

A mixture of peoples

One of the features of Brazil today is its very mixed population. For centuries, the country's only inhabitants were Amerindian tribes living in the Amazon basin. Following the Portuguese conquest in 1500, many other people from all over the world settled in Brazil and intermarried. The result is that Brazilians today are descended from many different peoples, including Portuguese settlers, native Indians, slaves from Africa, as well as migrants from Europe, the Far East, and the Middle East.

Soccer is a national obsession in Brazil, bringing together all ages and all sections of society.

Landscape and climate

Brazil is a country of vast distances and varied landscapes. In the north, it is dominated by the mighty Amazon River, which rises in the mountains of Peru and flows eastward to the Atlantic.

The basins

The Amazon Basin is like a huge bowl covering more than 3 million square miles (5 million square kilometers). Most of it is inside Brazil's borders and is covered in tropical rain forest. The Paraguay Basin formsa large, flat area in the Center-West of the country, where the rivers flow south into Paraguay, Uruguay, and Argentina. It includes an enormous, swampy region called the Pantanal, which is almost the size of France.

▶ An ancient tree in the Amazon rain forest near Manaus.

Facts at a glance

Land area: 3,265,077 sq. miles (8,456,510 sq. km)

Water area: 21,411 sq. miles (55,455 sq. km)

Highest point: Pico Neblina 9,888 feet (3,014 meters)

Coastline: 4,654 miles (7,491 km)

Longest river: The Amazon 4,300 miles (6,992 km) approx.

DID YOU KNOW? The Amazon pours out around 46 million gallons (210 million liters) of fresh water into the sea every day. The large island at the mouth of the Amazon, Marajo, is as big as Switzerland.

The coast

The Coastal Strip is almost 4,660 miles (7,500 km) long, but mostly less than 62 miles (100 km) wide. Its beautiful sandy beaches and natural harbors make it a popular tourist destination.

The highlands

The Guianan Highlands are in the north and stretch along the border with Venezuela and Guiana. They include Brazil's highest mountain, Pico Neblina.

The Brazilian Highlands are between 650–6,500 feet (200–2,000 meters) high and form a vast plateau roughly in the center of the country. Rivers flowing north from this region drain into the Amazon River. The mountains are not as high as the Guianan Highlands but still form a large physical barrier.

Climate

The Amazon Basin is hot and wet all year round with daytime temperatures averaging 79°F (26°C) and an annual rainfall of 59–98 inches (150–250 centimeters). The south of the country has a temperate climate with cool, wet winters and humid summers. Here, it can snow on the coldest winter days, and frosts can often destroy the coffee crop.

◭ The vast sand dunes at Maranhão on Brazil's northeast coast form lagoons during the rainy season at the start of each year.

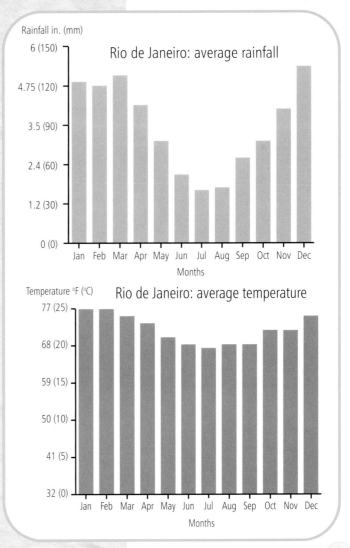

Population and health

Brazil's population today is the result of centuries of migration and intermarriage. The country's earliest inhabitants were Amerindian tribes living in the Amazon Basin. In the sixteenth century, millions of slaves were brought from Africa to work in Brazil's gold mines and plantations. Later, people from all over the world migrated to Brazil in search of better jobs and living conditions.

Migration and growth

After World Wars I and II, people from Europe and from countries such as China and Japan moved to Brazil in large numbers. Between 1970 and 2008, Brazil's population doubled to around 196 million. This was the result of natural population growth, but also because people continued to migrate to Brazil from overseas and from neighboring countries.

Facts at a glance

Total population:
196.3 million

Life expectancy at birth:
71.7 years

Children dying before age of 5: 2%

Ethnic composition:

White 53.7%
Mulatto and mestizo 39.1%
African and African-
  Amerindian 6.2%
Asian 0.5%
Amerindian 0.4%

▼ Children in Brazil today come from many different ethnic backgrounds.

Old and young

As the population has grown, the mix of old and young people has changed. There are now more people over 60, and the number of children under 14 is starting to fall as couples choose to have smaller families. However, Brazil still has a very young population compared to the United States and Europe.

Health

Brazilians generally are now living longer than ever before, and fewer children under five are dying of common diseases. This is mainly because there are more hospitals, and because doctors are using vaccines to prevent diseases from spreading. Brazilians today also have a better diet, with more protein to supplement traditional foods, such as rice and beans.

However, the contrast between rich and poor is extreme. In the northeast of the country, Brazil's poorest region, the child mortality rate is 60 per 1,000 births—double that of the wealthier southern and southeastern states.

⊙ A Pataxo Amerindian from Bahia, on Brazil's Atlantic coast.

DID YOU KNOW?
Brazil abolished slavery in 1888. In early 2008, however, the Brazilian government admitted to the United Nations that at least 25,000 Brazilians still live and work in slaverylike conditions.

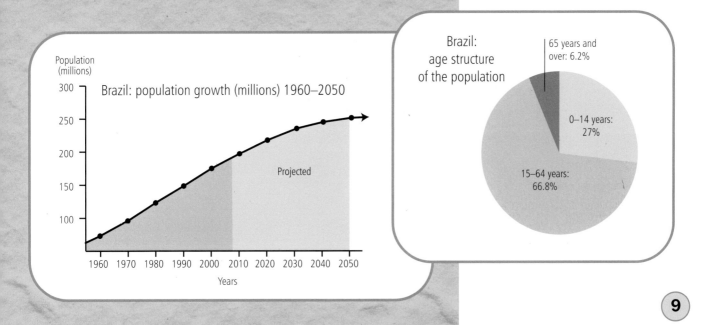

Population (millions)

Brazil: population growth (millions) 1960–2050

Projected

Years

Brazil: age structure of the population

65 years and over: 6.2%

0–14 years: 27%

15–64 years: 66.8%

Settlements and living

Since the 1960s, Brazil's cities have grown rapidly. Today, over 85 percent of Brazilians live in towns and cities, but the population is spread very unevenly around the country.

Population

Around 90 percent of all Brazilians live in the narrow Coastal Strip. This includes cities such as Rio de Janeiro, Recife, Salvador, and São Paulo. The state of São Paulo has a population density of 400 people per square mile (155 people per sq. km)—as high as many parts of Europe. The Amazon and Center-West are much less densely populated, with as few as 5 people per square mile (2 per sq. km).

Facts at a glance

Urban population:
85% (167 million)

Rural population:
15% (29.5 million)

Population of largest city:
18.8 million (São Paulo)

▼ High-rise apartment buildings dominate the skyline of São Paulo, Brazil's largest city.

Rich and poor

Some Brazilians are very rich and own several houses and even private jets. At the opposite extreme, many Brazilians in both the country and in urban areas lack clean water and other basic necessities of life.

Many of the urban poor live in slum areas known as *favelas*. Their homes are overcrowded and badly built and often have no water or electricity. The rural poor often live in remote villages in areas such as the Amazon and northeast. They survive by growing their own food on small plots of land and by hunting and fishing.

In rural areas of the south and southeast, farms are larger and mechanized. Many are owned and run by wealthy landowners. This region, the richest part of the country, produces approximately 60 percent of all Brazil's wealth.

The middle class

Between the extremes of rich and poor, Brazil has a growing middle class. These people are not wealthy, but they have good jobs and decent homes. They can also afford to send their children to good schools. Their standard of living is similar to that of middle-class Europeans or Americans.

◯ A home made from timber and palms in the Amazon rain forest.

DID YOU KNOW?
Brazil's cities are among the most dangerous in the world. Guns are one of the main causes of death for men in Rio, and in a 54-country survey, Brazil had the second-highest rate of deaths by firearms.

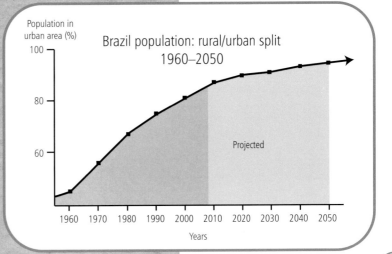

Population in urban area (%)

Brazil population: rural/urban split 1960–2050

100

80

60

Projected

1960 1970 1980 1990 2000 2010 2020 2030 2040 2050

Years

Family life

Family life in Brazil varies greatly from region to region. In poor rural areas of the Amazon Basin, large families live together in wooden shacks. In the cities of the south and southeast, middle-class people tend to live in apartment buildings and have small families.

Parents and grandparents

Most Brazilians are Roman Catholics and place a high value on family life. In many parts of the country, several generations of the same family live close to one another—often in the same house. Grandparents look after the children while the parents go out to work. Often the children work, too. But life in Brazil is changing, and the traditional extended family is no longer the only pattern.

▼ In rural areas of Brazil, families of six, eight, or even ten children are not unusual.

The role of women

In the past, Brazilian men were automatically seen as the head of the household, and women were expected to stay at home and care for the children. In 1988, women were given equal rights in law, and their status has improved in many ways. There are now as many girls as boys in Brazilian primary schools; more women are joining the workforce, and women are also taking jobs in law, medicine, engineering, and many other professions that were once open only to men.

◬ More Brazilian women are joining the workforce and studying for professional careers.

Living apart

More and more Brazilian families are having to live apart, as wage-earners head for the towns or cities in search of work. Sometimes men have to leave their families for weeks, even months at a time, in order to earn a living. Many families break up under the strain, and single-parent families are on the increase. Marriage is still the norm in Brazil, but people are getting married later in life than in the past, and the divorce rate is rising.

Family size

As people leave the country for towns in search of work, the size of the typical family has changed. In the country, where children help with work on the farms, families may still have six or eight children. In towns and cities, families are more likely to have just one or two children.

DID YOU KNOW?
In the Amazon rain forest, Yanomami Indian families live together in a single, oval-shaped building called a *shabono*. Yanomami settlements can contain anything from 50 to 400 people.

Religion and beliefs

Since the sixteenth century, Roman Catholicism has been Brazil's dominant religion. In total, around three-quarters of Brazilians are Catholics. A further 15 percent of the population are Protestant. This means that almost 90 percent of Brazil's population is Christian.

Other religions

Christianity was introduced to Brazil by Portuguese missionaries, but many of the other religions followed in Brazil today were introduced by immigrants and foreign settlers. In the northeast, more than a million people follow an African religion, Candomblé, which was brought to Brazil by slaves from Africa. There are also Muslims and Jews who are descended from immigrants from Middle Eastern countries such as Lebanon. More recently, large communities of Chinese and Japanese have introduced religions such as Buddhism and Shinto.

A Candomblé priest and priestess lead a carnival procession through the streets of a Brazilian town.

Indian religions

Before the Portuguese came to Brazil, the Amerindian tribes who had lived in the country for thousands of years followed their own religions. As well as honoring the spirits of their ancestors, the Indians worshiped plants, animals, and other rain forest spirits, and many of Brazil's native plants and animals have Indian names. There were once thought to be as many as 2–3 million Amerindians in Brazil. Today, only about 200,000 survive. Some still follow traditional beliefs, but many have converted to Catholicism.

Church and state

When Brazil gained independence from Portugal in 1890, the links between church and state were dissolved, and Catholicism ceased to be the country's official religion. However, the Catholic Church is still a powerful voice in Brazil. Over the last three decades, many Catholic priests and bishops have spoken out against poverty and injustice. Some have been persecuted and even murdered for supporting the rights of peasants and poor farmers.

⚪ Towering above Rio de Janeiro, the giant statue of Christ the Redeemer has a special importance for Brazilians and for Roman Catholics the world over.

DID YOU KNOW?
Followers of Candomblé believe that one all-powerful God, Oludumaré, is served by lesser gods called "orixas." Everyone has their own orixa that rules their destiny and acts as their protector.

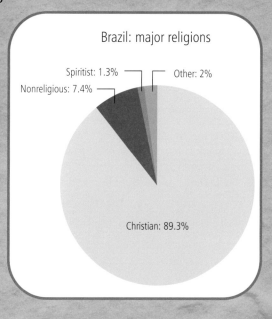

Brazil: major religions

Spiritist: 1.3%
Nonreligious: 7.4%
Other: 2%
Christian: 89.3%

Education and learning

In Brazil, it is compulsory for children between the ages of 7 and 14 to go to school. But despite the government providing school places for every child, there are many children who are not able to go to school, or who leave without finishing their basic schooling.

Missing school

Children living in poor rural areas may not be able to go to school because they live too far away and there are no buses or trains to take them there. Often, children are needed to help their parents on the farm. In the cities, children miss school because they have to earn money to support their families. It is not unusual to see school-age children selling goods on the streets of Brazil's towns and cities.

▼ These children attend a school in a remote village in Brazil's Amazon region.

State and private

Brazil has a system of state schools, but there are also private and church schools. Because there are so many young people in Brazil, providing education for everybody is a big challenge for the government. New schools are being built all the time, but buildings often have to be shared by more than one school, as well as being used by adult learners in the evenings. There are more schools in the cities than in the country, and parents often move to towns and cities in order to be near a good school for their children.

⬥ A construction worker at an adult literacy class in a Brazilian school.

Higher education

Attending Brazil's state-run colleges and universities is free, but to save living expenses, most students attend the one nearest their home so that they can continue to live with their family. Competition for entry to top public universities is often fierce, and in some classes, there can be as many as 200 applicants for every place.

There are many excellent private universities, but only wealthy families can afford to send their children there. Private language schools where children learn foreign languages, such as English, German, and French, are also popular with wealthy families.

DID YOU KNOW?
Some of the first schools in Brazil were founded by Catholic priests called Jesuits. Students who graduated from Jesuit schools often went on to study at Jesuit colleges in Portugal.

Employment and economy

Brazil is one of the wealthiest countries in South America and exports a huge range of products to countries all over the world. Together with Russia, India, and China, it is one of the world's fastest-growing developing economies. This group are known as the "BRIC" economies, after their first letters.

Industrialization

In the early twentieth century, Brazil's wealth came mainly from farming and mining, and most manufactured goods were imported. During World War II, the supply of goods from abroad was cut off. Because of this, the government began building up its own manufacturing industries, so that Brazil would not have to rely so heavily on imports.

The *Plano Real*

During the 1960s and 70s, Brazil's industries developed rapidly, but in the 1980s and 1990s, high levels of inflation slowed the country's growth. After several failed attempts to tackle the problem, the government introduced a scheme called the *Plano Real* in 1994. This brought stability and helped Brazil's economy to keep growing through the next decade.

> **Facts at a glance**
>
> **Contributions to GDP:**
>   Agriculture: 5.5%
>   Industry: 28.7%
>   Services: 65.8%
>
> **Labor force:**
>   Agriculture: 20%
>   Industry: 14%
>   Services: 66%
>
> **Female labor force:**
>   43.1% of total
>
> **Unemployment rate:** 9.3%

 The assembly line of a Brazilian aircraft factory.

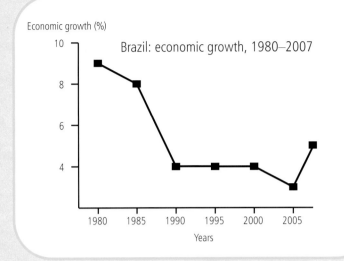

Economic growth (%)

Brazil: economic growth, 1980–2007

Years

Goods and services

Today, Brazil has the second-most advanced industrial sector in the Americas, with industries ranging from automobiles, steel, and petrochemicals to computers, aircraft, and consumer durables.

One of the most dramatic developments of the last ten years has been the growth in Brazil's service sector. Around two-thirds of Brazil's working population now have jobs in schools, hospitals, banks, and offices. Because of the growth of service industries, many people have left Brazil's rural areas for the cities, where most of the best-paid jobs are to be found.

Unemployment

Despite the growth of its economy, Brazil still suffers from high levels of corruption, violent crime, illiteracy, and poverty. Although there are many new jobs in Brazil, unemployment levels are high in both rural and urban areas, and the better jobs are more likely to be found in the southeast.

⬥ Staff and clients in a Brazilian hairdressing salon. Service sector jobs like hairdressing currently contribute 65.8% to Brazil's GDP.

Industry and trade

Brazil is richer in energy, minerals, timber, and other natural resources than almost any other country in the world. Products and raw materials from Brazil are traded with other countries such as the United States, China, Japan, and member countries of the European Union.

Mining and industry

Many of Brazil's most valuable natural resources are found underground. Minerals found in Brazil include bauxite (aluminum ore), copper and gold (used in computers and other electrical goods), asbestos (for building), diamonds (for industrial drills and jewelry) and chromium (used to make stainless steel). Brazil also has the world's biggest deposits of iron ore, the main raw material for making steel.

🔻 An open-pit gold mine at Pocone near Cuiaba, Pantanal, in the Paraguay Basin.

Some minerals are exported, but Brazil also uses minerals in its own industries to make products such as steel, cars and parts, trucks, planes, industrial chemicals, and machinery.

Energy

Brazil has its own coal, and oil has been discovered off the Atlantic coast near Rio de Janeiro. But the country's best source of energy is water. Brazil has more fresh water flowing through it than any other country on earth. This is used to generate electricity known as hydroelectric power, or HEP. Brazil already has many HEP stations, including the second-largest in the world at Itaipu, on the Paraná River.

⬤ A hydroelectric dam at the head of the Tocantins River in Goias state.

Imports and exports

In the 1950s, Brazil's main exports were raw materials and foods such as coffee and sugar. Major imports were manufactured goods, such s televisions, cars, and processed foods.

Today, nearly three-quarters of Brazil's exports are manufactured goods, such as shoes, vehicles, machinery, and processed foods. Brazil also imports materials and parts for goods that are produced locally. Some of these goods are then exported to other countries.

Brazil: major export partners

Netherlands: 4.3%
Germany: 4.4%
Argentina: 8.3%
China: 9.2%
U.S.A.: 14.2%
Other: 59.6%

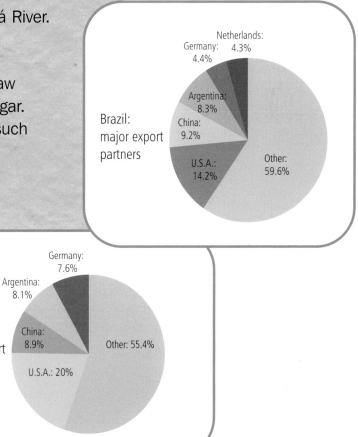

Brazil: major import partners

Germany: 7.6%
Argentina: 8.1%
China: 8.9%
U.S.A.: 20%
Other: 55.4%

Farming and food

Brazil has huge agricultural resources, and roughly a quarter of its working population are employed on farms and plantations. It is the world's largest producer of sugar cane and coffee, and its cocoa, soybeans, orange juice, tobacco, and tropical fruits and nuts are exported all over the world. Brazil is also a major meat producer and has more cattle than any other country—134,400,000 in 2004.

Types of farming

The southern part of the country is where most of Brazil's grains, oil seeds, and export crops are grown. In the southeast and Center-West, wheat, soybeans, coffee, and beans are produced on a massive scale using tractors and combine harvesters. In the temperate parts of the south, the soils and climate are better for smaller-scale production. Crops include grapes and potatoes, and these areas are famous for their dairy products.

Facts at a glance

Farmland: 8.2% of total land area

Main agricultural exports: soybeans, chicken, beef, coffee

Main agricultural imports: wheat, rubber, malt barley, rice

Average daily calorie intake: 3,060 calories

▼ Large-scale mechanized soybean farming in the southeast of Brazil.

Central Brazil contains vast areas of grassland with only scattered trees. The grasslands are less fertile than those of North America and are generally more suited for grazing than growing.

In the northeast, huge sugar plantations employ tens of thousands of people, often on very low wages. There are also many small farms where the farmers can barely grow enough to feed their families. The Amazon rain forest is poor farmland, but huge areas have been cleared for cattle ranching and soybeans. Fishing is also important here and along the northeast coast.

A farmer and his children on a sugar cane plantation in northern Brazil.

Land reform

Ownership of land in Brazil is very unequally divided. A few wealthy landowners own huge estates, but most peasants have no land of their own and have to rent small plots in return for a share of the harvest. The government has often promised land reform, but has usually preferred to fund large-scale industrial projects.

Diet

Much of the child mortality in Brazil is linked to malnutrition. The typical Brazilian diet consists of beans, rice, fruit, and *farinha*, a type of coarse flour. This is boosted by whatever meat or fish may be available. Average daily calorie intake is over 3,000 (similar to Europe), but this hides the fact that millions of Brazilians have poor diets and lack essential vitamins.

DID YOU KNOW? Brazil nut trees cannot be grown in plantations, so the nuts that we eat in chocolate bars and muesli have to be collected by hand from trees that grow wild in the rain forest.

Transportation and communications

In a country as big and varied as Brazil, traveling from place to place is often difficult. Wealthy Brazilians can afford to travel by plane, but most ordinary Brazilians have to drive or go by bus.

Road transportation

Brazil has the fourth-largest road network in the world, but less than 6 percent of its roads are paved with asphalt. The best roads are in the southeast, around the cities of São Paulo, Rio de Janeiro, and Belo Horizonte.

In 1970, the government launched an ambitious plan to drive a 2,000-mile (3,200-km) road called the Trans-Amazonian Highway through the Amazon forest, so that peasants from the crowded northeast of Brazil could settle the land. However, building the road was much more difficult than expected, and it was never completed. The result has been massive cost and long-term environmental damage to the region.

Railroads and air travel

Brazil has the tenth-largest railroad network in the world, but compared to the roads, trains carry few passengers and goods. They are mainly used for transporting minerals from the mining and industrial areas. Brazil's network

○ Traffic congestion on the outskirts of Rio de Janeiro.

Facts at a glance

Total roads: 1,088,560 miles (1,751,868 km)

Paved roads: 59,871 miles (96,353 km)

Railroads: 18,203 miles (29,295 km)

Major airports: 32

Major ports: 7

of 32 airports allows access to many parts of the country that are difficult to reach by road or train. At least half of these airports are big enough to handle international flights. There are also many smaller airfields that can be used by light aircraft and planes carrying freight.

Boats

In the Amazon region, people travel mainly by boat. Here, many towns and cities are difficult to reach by road, especially during the wet season. Boats vary from dugout canoes made from hollowed-out tree trunks, to overcrowded ferries and luxury air-conditioned boats for tourists.

Telephones and Internet

Over 100 million Brazilians now have cell phones, and networks are spreading rapidly. Internet use is also growing fast—Brazil has the fifth-highest number of Internet users in the world.

⬥ A cable car carries sightseers to the top of Rio de Janeiro's Sugar Loaf Mountain.

DID YOU KNOW?
Brazil was one of the first countries to install trolley cars in a major city. Trolleys were first introduced in Rio de Janeiro in 1859 and are still running in the city almost a century and a half later.

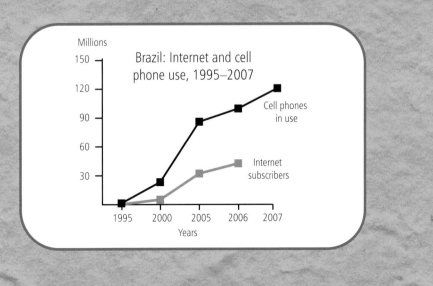

Millions

Brazil: Internet and cell phone use, 1995–2007

150

120

90

60

30

Cell phones in use

Internet subscribers

1995 2000 2005 2006 2007

Years

Leisure and tourism

Brazil's varied cultural life reflects the mix of ethnic groups that make up the country's population. Religious and cultural festivals take place throughout the year, and Brazil's dazzling carnivals attract visitors from all over the world.

Carnival

The annual Brazilian carnival season usually falls in February, which is the hottest time of year. Parties are held in every town and village, and normal life comes to a standstill as parades and processions block the streets. The most famous carnival takes place in Rio de Janeiro, when huge crowds watch Rio's top "samba schools" compete for the title of Carnival champion in the city's specially built "Sambadrome."

Sports and recreation

Brazil is one of the world's great sports nations, and soccer is played everywhere, from Amazonian villages to the huge Maracana stadium in Rio de Janeiro. Brazil has won the World Cup five times, more than any other team.

Facts at a glance

Tourist arrivals (millions)	
1995	2.0
2000	5.3
2005	5.4
2006	5.0
2007	5.0

Spectacular costumes and dancing make Rio's annual carnival one of the greatest shows in the world.

Brazilians also enjoy tennis, volleyball, sailing, and *capoeira* (right). Horseracing and motor racing are popular spectator sports, and millions watch the televized Brazilian Formula 1 Grand Prix, held at São Paulo's Interlagos circuit each year.

Music and literature

The music most often associated with Brazil is the *samba* and *bossa nova*, but many other regional forms, such as *frevo*, a fast, upbeat dance music, are also popular within Brazil itself.

Among the first Brazilian artists to achieve worldwide acclaim were the composer Hector Villa-Lobos (1887–1959) and the singer Carmen Miranda (1909–55). More recently, the novelist Paulo Coelho (*The Pilgrimage*, 1987) and filmmaker Fernando Cerelles (*City of God*, 2002) have also become internationally important figures.

Tourism

Tourism in Brazil is a growth industry, and in the summer, the beaches are crowded with people sunbathing, playing volleyball, jogging, and taking part in water sports. In 2008, Brazil was ranked the second-most attractive tourist destination in Latin America after Mexico.

⬤ Capoeira, a cross between slow-motion kick-boxing and dance, was originally brought to Brazil by African slaves.

DID YOU KNOW? The Maracana soccer stadium in Rio de Janeiro is the largest in the world. It was built for the 1950 World Cup Finals when 175,000 people watched the final between Brazil and Uruguay.

⬤ Copacabana Beach, Rio de Janeiro.

Environment and wildlife

Each of Brazil's landscapes is home to countless rare plants and animals. The most famous is the Amazon rain forest, which is believed to contain over 2.5 million insect species alone. Because of human activity, however, many of Brazil's species and ecosystems are now under threat.

Forests

The Amazon rain forest is the largest in the world, but is gradually being destroyed to make way for mines, roads, and farmland. In 2004 alone, 10,590 sq miles (27,429 sq km) of forest was destroyed—an area larger than Israel. Much of the rain forest has been replaced by fields of soybeans and huge cattle ranches. The tropical Atlantic forests that once ran almost the whole length of Brazil's coastline are also being replaced by sugar cane plantations and other large farms.

Facts at a glance

Proportion of area protected: 3.9%

Biodiversity (known species): 58,505

Known endangered species: 575

▼ Since 2000, more than 61,775 sq miles (160,000 sq km) of Amazon forest has been destroyed. The Brazilian government currently aims to cut deforestation to zero by 2015.

DID YOU KNOW? As well as destroying plant and animals, rain forest destruction also contributes to greenhouse gas emissions. When land use is taken into account, Brazil is the fourth-largest CO_2 emitter on the planet.

Endangered species

Countless plants and animals are facing extinction. In the Amazon, the wild hyacinth macaw, a rare type of parrot, now numbers less than 3,000. At even greater risk is a small monkey called the Golden Lion Tamarin. Just 2,000 of these animals live in the remaining areas of Atlantic forest. Even the tree that gave Brazil its name, Pau-Brasil, is almost extinct in the wild. The government has set up national parks to try and protect wildlife, but these cover less than 4 percent of the country. Several organizations such as WWF-Brazil run smaller projects to protect rare species and threatened animal habitats.

◯ The Brazilian jaguar is among many native species threatened with extinction.

Pollution

In the towns and cities, polluted air and water caused by chemicals, fumes, and waste is a major threat to human health. The government is trying to reduce pollution by encouraging cleaner sources of energy, such as ethanol for cars and hydroelectric power for generating electricity. There are also penalties for companies who pollute the environment.

▶ Pollution from factories is a serious threat to human health in many of Brazil's industrial areas.

Glossary

Amerindians Brazil's earliest-known inhabitants. At the time of European discovery, Amerindians were mostly seminomadic tribes who lived by hunting, fishing, gathering, and migrant agriculture

calorie intake way of measuring how much people eat. A calorie is a unit of food energy

cash crop crop that can be bought and sold for money

cattle ranching type of large-scale cattle farming that originated in the western U.S.A. and Canada

compulsory something that must be done

deforestation clearing away forest, usually to make way for large-scale farming or development

export good or service that is sold to another country

extinction when a species dies out or ceases to exist

federal republic system of government in which regions or states in a country are partly self-governing, but elect representatives to make decisions for them at national level. Republics do not have a king or queen as head of state.

fertile good for growing plants and crops

freight cargo carried by a commercial plane or ship

GDP total value of goods and services produced by a country

hydroelectric power electricity generated by harnessing the power of water. Hydroelectric power is the most widely used form of renewable energy.

illiteracy not being able to read or write

import good or service that is bought from another country

inflation when the price of goods and services in a country is rising

intermarriage marriage between members of different ethnic groups

malnutrition condition caused by lack of essential foods and vitamins

migration movement of people from one area or country to another, usually in search of work and better living conditions

mineral solid substance that is found in rocks or the ground. Salt, gold, and limestone are examples of minerals.

missionaries people who travel to other countries to preach Christian beliefs

natural resources water, soil, trees, and minerals that are found naturally in an area

plateau large, flat area of raised land

pollution poisoning or contaminating the environment with harmful chemicals

population density number of people living in an area, usually measured in persons per square mile or kilometer

raw materials resources such as timber and iron ore that are used to make products or other materials

renewable resource material that can restock itself so long as it is not over-harvested, for example, timber

service sector part of the economy that provides services such as banking, retail, education, and healthcare

state schools schools that are funded by the taxpayer and run by the government

temperate type of climate with mild summers and winters. Temperate climates can vary unpredictably.

vitamins substances found in food that are essential to human health

Topic web

Use this Topic Web to explore Brazilian
themes in different areas of study.

History
Find out about the
Portuguese conquest of
Brazil. What did the first
European explorers and
settlers hope to discover in
South America?

Geography
Discuss why almost all the
main cities in Brazil are
within 62 miles (100 km)
of the Atlantic coast. Why
do you think the northeast
of the country has
remained so poor?

Science
Brazil's huge rivers and
waterways are a vital
source of hydroelectric
power. What do you think
are the advantages of
generating energy in
this way?

Maths
Find out how many
Brazilian Real (R$) there
are in $1. Choose some
items (e.g. a bottle of
water, an apple) and work
out how much they would
cost in Brazilian money.

Brazil

English
Write a story about the
thoughts and feelings of a
sixteenth-century European
explorer on meeting an
Amerindian tribesman from
the Brazilian rain forest for
the very first time.

Citizenship
Many people in Brazil are
poor. What do we mean
when we use the word
"poverty"? Create a spider
diagram to explore what
you understand
by poverty.

**Design and
Technology**
One of Brazil's most
important exports is rubber.
Make a list of all the
everyday things around your
home that are made of
rubber. What do you think
people used before rubber
was available?

**Information
Technology**
Use the Internet to find
out when is the best time
to vacation in Brazil
and what are the main
things to see.

Further Information, Web Sites, and Index

Further reading

Brazil: The Culture by Malika Hollander (Crabtree Publishing Company, 2003)
Destination Detectives: Brazil by Ali Brownlie Bojang (Raintree, 2007)
Kids Around the World: We Live in Brazil by Francois-Xavier Freland and Sophie Duffet
(Abrams Books for Young Readers, 2007)

Web Sites

Due to the changing nature of Internet links, PowerKids Press has
developed an online list of Web sites related to the subject of this book.
This site is updated regularly. Please use this link to access this list:
http://www.powerkidslinks.com/discovc/brazil/

Index

Amazon River 6, 7
Amazon *see* rain forest
Amerindians 5, 8, 9, 15

Bahia 9
Belo Horizonte 24
boats 25
Brasilia 4, 5
Buddhism 14

Candomblé 14, 15
capoeira 27
carnival 26
children 12, 13, 16–17
cities 10, 11, 13, 17, 19, 29
climate 6–7
Coastal Strip 4, 7, 10, 28
coffee 7, 22
computers 19, 25
crime 4, 19

diet 9, 23
divorce 13

economy 5, 18–19
ethnic diversity 5, 8, 26
exports 4, 18, 20, 21, 22

family 12–13
favela 11

fishing 11, 23
food 21, 22–23

government 4, 17, 23, 24

health 9
hydroelectric power (HEP) 21

immigration 5, 8, 14
imports 18, 19, 21
inflation 18

Jesuits 17

land ownership 23
landscape 6–7
literacy 16, 17

malnutrition 23
manufacturing 18, 19, 20–21
middle class 11
Middle East 5, 14
mining *see* natural resources
mountains 7
movies 27
music 27

natural resources 4, 8, 18, 20–21, 23

Pantanal 6
Peru 6
Pico Neblina 7
Plano Real 18
pollution 28, 29
population (mix) 5, 8, 9, 10, 26
ports 5
Portugal 4, 5, 14, 17
poverty 4, 9, 11, 12, 15

rain forest 6, 11, 13, 15, 23, 24, 28–29
Recife 10
religion 12, 14–15, 17, 26
Rio de Janeiro 10, 15, 24, 25, 26, 27
Roman Catholicism 12, 14, 15, 17
rural life 11, 12, 13, 16, 19

samba 26, 27
São Paulo 10, 24
school 13, 16–17, 19
service sector 19
shabono 13
Shinto 14
slavery 5, 8, 9, 14
soccer 5, 26, 27

soybeans 22
sports 26–27
sugar cane 19, 21, 23, 28

tourism 27
transportation 5, 16, 24–25
Trans-Amazonian Highway 24

unemployment 19
university 17

wealth 11, 17, 23, 24
wildlife 15, 29
women 13
work 13, 19, 22, 23

Yanomami indians 13

DISCARD